Denise Pereira Alves de Sena

Ageing

Denise Pereira Alves de Sena

Ageing

A psychoanalytical view

ScienciaScripts

Imprint

Cover image: www.ingimage.com

This book is a translation from the original published under ISBN 978-613-9-61468-4.

Publisher:
Sciencia Scripts
is a trademark of
Dodo Books Indian Ocean Ltd. and OmniScriptum S.R.L publishing group

120 High Road, East Finchley, London, N2 9ED, United Kingdom
Str. Armeneasca 28/1, office 1, Chisinau MD-2012, Republic of Moldova, Europe
Printed at: see last page
ISBN: 978-620-7-63093-6

Table of contents:

Dedication

I dedicate this book to my beloved maternal grandmother Maria do Carmo Lopes, who is now 97 years old.

All lives

Inside me lives a cabocla with an evil eye Huddled

at the foot of the dunghill looking into the fire

Bless a broken heart, put a spell on it

Ogum, Orixá, macumba, warrior, Ogan, pai de santo.

The washerwoman from the Red River lives inside me

Her delicious smell of water and soap

Clothespin, bundle of clothes, indigo stone

Her green crown from Sao Caetano.

The woman cook lives inside me

Peppers and onions, well-made delicacies, clay pots

, wood-fired Taipa, old black kitchen,

well curled with Picuma, pointed stone, coconut cumbuco,

stepping on garlic and salt.

The woman of the people lives inside me

Very proletarian, very loud-mouthed

Unabashed, unprejudiced, thick-skinned In

flip-flops and with children.

The woman from the country lives inside me, grafted from the earth, half

Casmurra, hard-working, early riser, illiterate With

her feet on the ground, well-birthed, well-bred,

her twelve children, her twenty grandchildren.

The woman of life lives inside me, my little sister,

So despised, so mumbled, pretending to be happy about her sad fate.

All the lives inside me in my life

The mere life of the obscure.

Cora Coralina, aged 76.

INTRODUCTION

The ageing of the world's population has been a much-discussed phenomenon over the last decade. Medical progress, technological advances and a strong trend towards lower birth rates have all contributed to this. Costa (1998, p.15) points out that "we are in the midst of the 'Age of Ageing', a period that runs from 1975 to 2025, according to the United Nations Organization".

According to data from the 2000 Census, the Brazilian population at the time was estimated at approximately 169,500,000 inhabitants, of which 15.5 million were aged 60 or over. However, the increase in life expectancy in Brazil has not been accompanied by public health policies capable of meeting the demands generated by the elderly population. Localized pain, inability to move, loneliness, abandonment, physical and mental illness, long periods of retirement, among other factors, are all present in the lives of people over 60. In order to correct these distortions, modern society has the task of providing active and healthy ageing, valuing autonomy and preserving the physical and emotional independence of the elderly.

Society in the 21st century is looking for ways to keep up with this "living longer" in a variety of ways: specific public policies are being created, more appropriate names are being sought for this phase, such as "third age", "good age", "happy age" and "best age", laws are being drawn up to provide preferential care, old age has become a segment in the tourism market, in gyms and at social events such as balls, bingos and parties. All these quotes illustrate how people over 60 are clamoring for personalized attention.

Different types of knowledge that research ageing indicate that this phase has always belonged to two very different places: that of being wise or that of being a hindrance. Sometimes old age is accompanied by a sense of recognition and wisdom, and sometimes it is uselessness and "cost" that prevail, as people become incapable of producing. Kamkhagi (2008, p.25) points out that "in both prehistoric and ancient societies, the same contradictions existed in relation to growing old, which have been found as a constant throughout history: the elderly are seen and adored as wise, or execrated as a nuisance".

In the field of psychology and psychoanalysis, old age is still a little-researched topic. According to Kamkhagi (2008, p.15) "there are surprisingly few psychoanalytic studies dedicated to the ageing process". This stage of human development seems to be neglected by psychology which, in this area, only values and studies degenerative and mental illnesses. But what about the subjective and emotional pain that accompanies the elderly? In analysis, when an elderly person speaks, what is heard? Old age? Neurosis? Depression? Wisdom?

The "father of psychoanalysis", Sigmund Freud, did not study the extremes of human development - childhood and old age. Child analysis was studied by important followers with research and great discoveries as described in the works of Melaine Klein and Winnicott. However, old age was also forgotten by the post-Freudians.

Brink (1983, p.61) points out that "Freud had a rather negative view of the possibilities for psychoanalysis to succeed with the elderly, complaining that people over 40 were no longer educable, and that the mass of material to deal with was simply too much".

Mucida (2006, p.25), an analyst who has worked with the elderly, states that "psychoanalysis has so far shown little interest in this issue, either because it considers the elderly to be adults like the others, not distinguishing a differentiated clinic in old age, or because of Freud's legacy". This phase was not her object of study. And the author continues "(...) of all the contraindications or limits pointed out by Freud regarding the efficacy of analysis, only old age remains silent" (MUCIDA, 2006, p.15).

As a current topic with little literature and academic research, old age is imposing itself and forcing various professional fields to rethink their approach to this phase of human development. This research is justified by the need to bring psychoanalysis into contact with this scenario - growing old. If it succeeds in its aim, this work could contribute to the construction of specific academic knowledge on this subject.

The general aim of this monographic study is therefore to construct a possible relationship between narcissism and ageing. In order to achieve this, the author has chosen the following specific objectives:

- Relate the concept of Narcissism and the Oedipus Complex to ageing;
- Understanding the relationship between old-age depression and narcissism, and..,
- To help build an understanding of this now valued phase of life - ageing.

The methodology for this work will be bibliographical research, with a theoretical basis in Freudian psychoanalytic concepts.

This monographic study is divided into three chapters:

Chapter 1- "The old in society" - consists of a brief historical survey of the role of the old in society, as well as a discussion of Sigmund Freud's old age.

Chapter 2- "Psychoanalytic concepts" - aims to define and relate two central themes of the constitution of the self, for psychoanalytic theory, relating them to the aging process: Narcissism and the Oedipus Complex.

Chapter 3- "Ageing and depression" - this chapter aims to discuss depression as one of the possibilities for the self in ageing.

And in the conclusion, the author articulates the concepts presented in the aforementioned chapters and ends by pointing out the need to continue psychoanalytic studies on ageing.

Chapter 1

1 THE OLD IN SOCIETY

Without the aim of fully describing the construction of the old over time in society, this chapter is intended only as a brief history. It should be made clear that the terms "old" and "elderly" will be used to identify people over the age of 60, as synonyms, and without the intention of arousing any kind of prejudice. The physical condition involved in this stage of human development will not be addressed here.

Throughout human history, the elderly in society have played different roles and occupied different places in the social imagination. They have been labeled in different ways: wise, demented, a nuisance, disposable, among others. According to Kamkhagi (2008, p.22) "(...) the conceptions of old age that are known from literature sometimes place the elderly in a masterful place, sometimes in a space of decrepitude". Freud's "Totem and Taboo" illustrates the wise place occupied by the elderly in the Australian aboriginal tribe, "(...) common matters are decided by a council of elders" (1914/1996, v. XIII, p. 23).

In fact, what marks this place are: the culture, social and economic relations in force at the time. As Kamkhagi (2008, p.22) points out, "the place of the old, throughout this historical process, goes beyond subjective reality and involves symbolic aspects that are fixed by culture". Simone Beauvoir (*apud* MUCIDA, 2006, p.64) points out that "(...) when the climate is harsh, the circumstances difficult, the resources insufficient, the old age of men often resembles that of animals", in other words, the elderly, weak and debilitated, are abandoned by their flocks.

The lack of historical material providing precise information on the *status quo of* the old man in ancient societies is a relevant factor in this investigation. The inferences made are based on ethnographic material from 19th and 20th century tribes found by anthropologists. There is evidence that the elders of the time, whose age ranged from 25 to 35, enjoyed privileges due to their longevity and supposed wisdom (KAMKHAGI, 2008).

Mucida (2006, p.65) cites poor communities such as the Koriaks, Chukchees and Incas where family relationships were close and respectful, "property was distributed among the elderly and they ran the camp". Among the Yahgans, the most primitive people known, with no religion, no utensils of any kind, nomads, starving and living a very precarious life, the old man had the best place in the hut and was served first at meals.

The role of sage can be justified by the fact that those societies were agraphic, also known as "oral societies", meaning that the elders held the knowledge and know-how. Therefore, only they could "pass on" culture and history to younger people, as they were judges, guardians, sorcerers or witches with power. However, if growing old was accompanied by dementia, they tended to be seen as nuisances, not worthy of reverence. However, it is likely that in this dichotomous view of the old - wise and a nuisance - the image of the magician prevailed, the prestige that longevity conferred on them (KAMKHAGI, 2008).

This role as guardian of knowledge probably declined with the emergence and dominance of writing. Its memory lost its importance. Knowledge could be passed on to new generations without the need for the old man to exist. It is possible to suppose that at this time in the development of society, the image of the decrepit, decayed and lapsed old man began to emerge, as a "burden" on nomadic groups in the face of the scarcity of resources and the harshness of everyday life.

It's important to note that there was a gender issue to consider. In those societies, the old woman was allowed to be part of a group that she hadn't "circulated" in before, which was only for men. Thus, at the menopause, she would be liberated and would have greater autonomy over her life, since by not menstruating, she would no longer represent a "danger". In this sense, both elderly women and men are seen as wise, as if it was only at this stage of life that women became equal in importance to men. Even so, the place of decadence, of the ugly, fearful and sick old woman goes hand in hand with wisdom.

However, these statements are only suppositions. Only with the material left behind by societies that mastered writing is it possible to observe accounts that reveal the construction of different images of the old. Minois (*apud* KAMHAGI, 2008, p.25) quotes an excerpt from an anguished testimony from Egypt, dated 4500 BC:

> How painful the end of an old man is! They grow weaker every day, their eyesight diminishes and their ears become deaf, their strength is lacking and their heart no longer rests, they become silent and no longer speak. His intellectual faculties diminish and it is impossible to remember today what happened yesterday. Every bone aches. Tasks that were done with enthusiasm a moment ago are only carried out with difficulty and even the sense of taste disappears. Old age is the worst evil that can afflict a man.

It is possible to conclude that, even at that time when life expectancy was not so long, aging already frightened people, showing their finitude and decay, both physically and subjectively.

In ancient China, where power was centralized and authoritarian, society was based on the family and obedience to elders, since the culture required more experience than strength in the struggle for survival. According to Confucius (*apud* MUCIDA, 2006, p.67):

> At 15, I applied myself to the study of wisdom; at 30, I consolidated it; at 40, I had no more debts; at 60, there was nothing left in the world that could shock me; at 70, I could follow the desires of my heart without transgressing the moral law.

Kamkhagi (2008) also describes various rituals known throughout history that illustrate how the elderly have played different fundamental roles in social construction:

- In the 5th century BC, the Massageta people had the habit of immolating the healthy elderly, a ritual performed by the whole family, who, after cooking the body of the immolated, ate its flesh in search of wisdom;
- The Mongol Turks only respected and cared for the healthy elderly; the sick were left to fend for themselves;
- There is evidence that African and indigenous tribes eliminated their elderly for economic reasons and even as a germ of denial of old age, a search for eternal youth and avoidance of finitude.

Mucida (2006) highlights those tribes whose custom is to abandon their elders, leading them to huts far from the villages, abandoning them to death: the Chukchees (Siberia), the Bushmen (South Africa) and the Eskimos of Angmassalik (Groelancia).

Kamkhagi (2008) also gives an overview of the old man throughout history, which she considers relevant to quote in this work:

a) The old man in the Hebrew world:

There is evidence that in Jewish culture the elderly were idolized, "...old age among the Hebrews was seen as a reward for obedience to God, as a virtue"

(KAMKHAGI, 2008, p.26). The Hebrew family that did not have an old man would not be blessed.

The Old Testament, an instrument for organizing this society, idolizes Jacob and Methuselah (who lived for hundreds of years), ratifying the aforementioned evidence - admiration for the old. "The old were highly valued and praised by Jehovah, who appointed them as his spokesmen" (KAMKHAGI, 2008, p.26).

In this society, the elders were part of the Assembly of the Elders, in the field of justice, politics and religion "whose function was to organize and decide on all matters concerning their communities" (KAMKHAGI, 2008, p.26). The Sanhedrin, the highest body of the Hebrew people, was made up of 70 elders of the people - illustrious men whose daughters could only marry priests.

The Bible generally praises the elderly. It considers gray hair a crown of glory and wrinkles a mark of distinction. In the commandment that says "You shall honor Father and Mother" there is a strong indication of how "sinful" it is to mistreat old people, and such an act is punishable by God.

Mucida (2006, p.67) points out that "the biblical accounts are not homogeneous. There are some that boast about old age and others that, on the contrary, make it a shame".

According to Minois (*apud* KAMKHAGI, 2008), it wasn't until the 10th century BC that literature began to be less emphatic about the idealized role of the old. The first writings began to appear about the natural burden attributed to old age - physical pain and diminished capacities. At the same time, the value of the elderly began to be relativized in a slow, slight but perceptible way.

Kamkhagi (2008) points out that, according to researchers from antiquity, the great reflection on growing old is to be found in the "Book of Job". In it, the foundations that supported the prestige of the elderly are questioned. For example: men grow old regardless of their character (good or bad) and not everyone becomes wise and intelligent. The deconstruction of the image of the guardian of wisdom or the recipient of God's favor begins.

Hellenic thought began to treat old age as a decadent period of life, with the old man being devoid of desires and incapable of feeling carnal pleasures. It was at this time of conflict over the image of the old man within Jewish society that the work "Tamulde" appeared - one of the works that governed the life of the Jewish people. It reiterates the need to respect the elderly, pointing to the social and spiritual concern with old age.

b) The old in Greek culture:

In many ways, Greek culture represented changes in Western civilization, especially with regard to the arts, theater, literature, politics, aesthetics, philosophy and the awakening to the power of beauty and youth. In this culture, the old lost even more of their value, or established an exchange - beauty for wisdom.

The Greek devotion to beauty causes a definitive schism between youth and old age. Old age is degenerative and ugly. Death could represent something honorable and more valuable than "wise" aging. For the Greeks "(...) the ideal, according to mythology itself, was eternal youth" (KAMKHAGI, 2008, p.30).

Often in mythology, the old man appears as a hateful figure. The struggle between young and old, sons and fathers, was the inspiration for several Greek myths.

When he was young, Kronos took revenge on his father Uranus by cutting off his testicles while he slept; in adulthood, Kronos devoured his descendants so that the prophecy that one of them would destroy him would not be fulfilled; Zeus, Kronos' son, kills him and frees gods and goddesses from the punishments imposed by Kronos... In short, the myths portray how difficult it is for the old to accept the new generations, the need for the young to destroy the old and how cruel the old are (COSTA, 1998).

Mucida points out that in ancient Greece, old age was generally associated with honor: Gera and géron are words that designate advanced age and also the privileges of age - the right to eldership and the delegation of duties. "For Homer, it is associated with wisdom. In contrast to this idea ... there is also horror ... loss of physical strength, changes in image, loss of power..." (MUCIDA, 2006, p. 68).

In an attempt to remain in power, the leader of the *Polis* maintained the Council of Geronts (28 members). Here the elders were respected by the young, who would not be able to reach the most important positions, only with the passage of time. An idea of wisdom is maintained by this Council. However, for Greek society, and for those it influenced, the decrepitude of old age is undeniable. Wisdom is a possibility, but the loss of youth is a relevant and undeniable fact (KAMKHAGI, 2008).

c) The old man in the Roman world:

Roman law gave the old man the figure of *pater* e *mater familias,* which guaranteed him financial powers over the other family members. In other words, the other family members would have to wait for the death of the eldest to administer the estate. This guaranteed privileges to the elderly and, at the same time, provoked anger among family members who were at the mercy of the old man's wishes.

With the passage of time, Roman laws changed and the old man returned to the dichotomous question: wise man or hindrance? The "Council" of the Romans was the Senate. It was mostly made up of older gentlemen.

Pessimism was already evident in the literature of the time. Minois (*apud* KAMKHAGI, 2008, p.33) quotes a satire by Juvenal:

> (...) old age is first and foremost that deformed, hateful, despicable face; instead of skin, an ugly breastplate, drooping cheeks, wrinkles similar to those that the monkey-mother rubs around her mouth... old people are all alike: their voice trembles like their legs; there is no hair on their polished skull; their nose drips like that of a child. The poor old man only has his toothless gums to chew his bread.

d) The old man in the High Middle Ages:

Since the Lower Middle Ages, around the year 1000, old age has completely lost its value. What matters here is physical strength to fight battles and work in the fields. "The only work of the time, on the land, was extremely coarse and heavy for the old individual, who was excluded from production" (KAMKHAGI, 2008, p.36). In this period, the old, regardless of their health or *status quo,* are always viewed in a very unfavorable light.

e) The old man at some important moments over the centuries:

- Eleventh century: Christianity helps build the image of the son who dethrones the father.

In every respect. The figure of the old man is becoming more and more forgotten and distant;

- 12th to 15th centuries: in general, there is little information about the old man. Society isn't really interested in the subject, not least because the

people lived an average of 30 years. Literature portrays the association between old age and decrepitude, as the Brothers Grimm (*apud* Mucida, 2006, p.69) illustrate with a tale:

> God had allotted 30 years of life for man to all the animals, the donkey, the dog and the monkey. They managed to get God to cut 18 years, 12 years and 10 years respectively from the number set. Man, on the other hand, asked for longevity, obtaining an extension of his age with the reductions given to the donkey, the dog and the monkey, totaling 70 years, without knowing that it would represent decrepitude. He would live fast until he was 30, the next 18 years he would live like a donkey, carrying others on his shoulders, the next 12 years like a dog, crawling from one corner to another, because he would have no teeth left to bite, and his last 10 years would be like a monkey; he would no longer have a good fit, he would do bizarre things, a bit weird, causing laughter.

- During the Renaissance, the accumulation of money was no longer a sin in the eyes of the Church, and the elderly began to occupy positions in society again. The economic rise of the bourgeoisie favors the elderly. In the Renaissance, some texts were dedicated to the idea of a "model" old age - a sober and regimented life. In contrast to this concept, there are also texts in which youth and beauty are the relevant aspects, producing a certain repugnance to the aging body, especially the female body. In Erasmus' text, the elderly woman is ridiculed and pleasure is censored, demonstrating how love and sexuality are forbidden terrain for the elderly (MUCIDA, 2008);
- With the Industrial Revolution, medical and health advances have helped to increase life expectancy and quality of life;
- 18th century - the elderly ceased to be a burden on society by learning a trade and contributing to industries.
- Over the course of the 19th century, longevity increased and old people began to regain their place in society. The accumulation of land and wealth gave the elderly some respect from the younger generation.

Nowadays, power relations between young and old are still tense.

Respect for our elders goes hand in hand with competition and the search for production space. The dichotomy between the wise and the hindrance is still present. In addition to all the social adversity experienced by this subject, there is also his own mourning: to lose health, beauty, social spaces, employability, among others, is to experience his own mourning, denying it, since it is always the other who grows old.

Since the 1980s, a number of commercial films have portrayed the conflicts of aging. Examples include:

- "Someone's got to give in" (Diane Keaton and Jack Nicholson/2003): the central theme is sexuality in the "fall" of life. Successful executive "Harry" (Jack Nicholson), over 60, who only dates pretty young women, is surprised to find himself in love with writer "Erica" (Diane Keaton), also over 60. Both initially resist, but when they give in to their desires, they (re)discover the new radiance of their bodies and the advantages of a mature love life.
- "Elsa & Fred - A love of passion" (China Zorrilla and Manuel Alexandre/2005): in this movie the characters are older (Elsa 82 years old and Fred 78 years old) and the central theme is "relationships". Elsa is chronically ill with kidney disease and Fred is a healthy widower. Both have children who want to control their lives because they have lost the ability to manage them. They fall in love, at Elsa's insistence, and (re)discover and (re)mean the small pleasures of life, despite their age.
- "My father, a lifelong connection" (Jack Lemmon, Ted Danson/1989): the movie deals with the relationship between father and son. In it, the old man becomes a sage who influences his son's life as he gets older. The successful businessman reluctantly quits his job to look after his ageing parents. Seeing his father plunged into senility, illness and loneliness, the son rethinks his own life and tries to make amends for lost

time.

f) The old Freud:

As this academic work is a psychoanalytic study, the author believes it is important to briefly comment on Sigmund Freud's life, highlighting his painful and productive old age.

Sigmund Freud was born on May 6, 1856 and died on September 23, 1939 at the age of 83. His parents adored him and his mother believed unconditionally in the potential of "my golden Siggy". Edmundson (2009, p. 157) comments that "... he had his own room in a small, crowded house, and everyone was warned not to make a sound while he was studying".

Freud always had a remarkable intelligence: he spoke five languages fluently (Italian, French, Spanish, English and German), read Shakespeare from the age of 8, drew very well and entered medical school at the age of 17. His passions included collecting works of art, antiques, statuettes, books, dogs and smoking cigars. In adulthood, he married Martha, had six children, grandchildren and created psychoanalysis (EDMUNDSON, 2009; BREGER, 2002).

From the age of 63, losses and bereavements were present in Freud's life. In 1919 he lost his daughter Sophie (26) who was pregnant with his third child, in 1923 he discovered cancer and buried his favorite grandson (Sophie's son) at the age of four, a victim of meningitis. Freud (*apud* MUCIDA, 2006, p.42) stated that "he represented all my children and grandchildren to me and, since his death, I no longer love my grandchildren and have no pleasure in living".

Cancer: at the age of 67, Freud discovered it and underwent successive surgeries (a total of 31), but he continued to produce and write his work. He "administered" the doses of medication in such a way as not to inhibit his capacity for thought. Goldfarb (1998, p.84) points out that "an enormous drive impelled him to continue working despite the difficulties and suffering".

On October 12, 1923, Freud fitted a prosthesis (which he called a "monster") which "was a gigantic, denture-like object designed to separate the mouth from the nasal cavity. It had to be removed at frequent intervals for cleaning, but removal was not easy, nor was reinsertion" (EDMUNDSON, 2009, p.170). Successive jaw infections resulted in deafness in Freud's right ear.

In 1926, precancerous lesions began to proliferate and each one had to be treated surgically, by electro-coagulation or a combination of painful procedures. Edmundson (2009, p. 171) states that:

> During all these years, Freud constantly felt pain, sometimes mild, sometimes moderate, sometimes more intense. His response to the pain was to take an aspirin, smoke another cigar and continue working. After almost every intervention, Freud would jump back into life: within a day or two, he was seeing patients or at his desk again.

Freud knew his frailty. In 1936, at the age of 80, he wrote to his friend, Lou-Andreas Salomé (*apud* MUCIDA, 2006, p.43), about his pessimism about old age: "I cannot get used to the miseries and helplessness of old age and I face, with a kind of nostalgia, the passage into nothingness".

1938, Hitler invades Vienna. Freud was 81 years old. He was aged, pale, bent over, with skin as thin as "rice paper", frail and very thin. His prosthetic jaw prevented him from speaking as firmly as before, but his gaze remained firm, determined and threatening to the *Führer* (EDMUNDSON, 2009; BREGER, 2002).

The Nazis persecuted him as best they could: they raided his publishing house, set fire to part of his work (in a public square), arrested his children (Anna and Martin) for questioning, levied extremely high taxes, visited his house and stole the money he had in the safe, confiscated his rich collection of art and books, as well as unspoken threats to the entire Freud family. However, Freud had influential friends such as the French princess Marie Bonaparte, Ernest Jones, US President Roosevelt, Albert Einstein and others. They all helped Freud and his children leave Vienna for London. However, Freud's four sisters were unable to leave and were murdered by the Nazis (EDMUNDSON, 2009; BREGER, 2002).

From the age of 60, even though he was physically weak and emotionally bereaved, the elderly Freud continued to produce and immortalize his work through his writings. To illustrate the rich intellectual output of this admirable man, the author cites the main titles of the texts contained in the "Brazilian Standard Edition of the Complete Psychological Works of Sigmund Freud", dated from 1916 onwards: The Stranger (1919), Beyond the Pleasure Principle (1920), The Ego and the Id (1923), Neurosis and Psychosis (1923/24), Unrest in Civilization (1929/30), Fetishism (1927), Endless Analysis (1937), Moses and Monotheism (1939). As well as other texts, including Brief Writings, Conferences, Letters and publications in newspapers and magazines.

In September 1939, when there were no more surgical resources available, the father of psychoanalysis decided to die at the age of 83. Mucida (2006, p.43) reports that:

> (...) in September 1939, in a state of total deterioration and protected by a mosquito net to avoid the terrible smell he exuded, Freud, in accordance with an agreement signed with Max Schur and his daughter Anna, asked him to put an end to this torture: 'two centigrams of morphine are enough to put Freud to sleep. The dose is repeated twelve hours later'. Freud falls into a coma

from which he will never awaken.

Freud "... represents a case of old age in which the passion for knowledge was superior to the destructive force of the dramatic situations he had to go through" (GOLDFARB, 1998, p.79).

His life is an important contribution to understanding that a normal old age is not necessarily one without pain, passions and losses. His tireless fight against his serious illness and old age is evidenced in his rich output after his 60th birthday.

The big question that remains for this author is: did all of Freud's rich output after the age of 60 have anything to do with the defense mechanism of denial - of illness and old age? This is one possibility in interpreting Freud's life. What is known is that he lived his last years on the run from the Nazis, managing his physical and subjective pain, and writing.

Chapter 2

2 PSYCHOANALYTIC CONCEPTS

In formulating his theory, Freud used Greek myths to explain the phenomena he observed. Two of them define the theory of the constitution of the self - Narcissism and the Oedipus Complex.

The baby's intrauterine life is supposed to be full of pleasures. It feeds, breathes, is cradled by its mother's walking and breathing and is protected from the adversities of the outside world. Throughout the 40 weeks of pregnancy, the baby suffers "some discomfort" during training contractions (false contractions or "Braxton-Hicks"). Other than that, just pleasure.

When labor begins, uterine contractions signal to the baby that the uterus is no longer the best place for him to stay: it's tight and oxygen only appears after the contraction. It's definitely best to change location. Garcia-Roza (2008, p.192) states that "the most archaic division, at the level of the individual, is that which results from birth (...) with the cutting of the umbilical cord, the individual is not only separated from his mother, but also loses part of himself. From that moment on, he is characterized as an incomplete, split being (...)".

After birth, the baby experiences the world through its caregiver, usually the mother. The symbiotic state in this duet is perceptible and necessary for the subject's development. Hornstein (2008, p.27) points out that "prematurity gives rise to something more than a lasting attachment of the child to the first objects of love: a never-quenched desire for fusion. In every adult there lingers this premature child who aspires to total union with the other".

The mother rescues her narcissistic desires when she gives birth and the baby begins to form its own self. Garcia-Roza (2008, p.193) explains that "having lost part of itself, the child will look for external objects to fill this lack. The one that first presents itself as capable of replacing the lost part is the mother's breast. It will be the first pulse object".

Freud, in the elaboration of his science, developed a theory about the functioning of the psychic apparatus, which would be governed by the principles of displeasure-pleasure. Násio (1999, p.16) summarizes this functioning by stating that "the principle that governs this path (of psychic energy)... is very clear: receive the energy, transform it into action and, consequently, reduce the tension in the circuit". In other words, the principle of displeasure-pleasure is the attempt by the circuit (psychic apparatus) to completely discharge internal tension (representing the pulses), seeking the inertia that would be absolute pleasure. In this way, pleasure would be the suppression of tension "resetting the system" and displeasure would mean maintaining or increasing tension. Therefore, the only organizing quality of the self is the pleasure-unpleasure that exists in the "mother-baby" pair.

Thus, it is in the relationship with the other that the baby begins the process of forming the self. "The psyche and the world meet and are born with each other, and the psychic apparatus is the result of this encounter" (GARCIA-ROZA, 2008, p.187).

2.1 Narcissism

Legend has it that Narcissus was a beautiful man who aroused desire in both men and women. Punished by Artemis, Narcissus fell in love only with himself, as quoted below

> ... Narcissus tried to embrace and kiss the beautiful young man he saw in front of him (reflected in the river), but gradually he realized that it was himself, and he remained enraptured for hours, contemplating his own image. How could he bear the fact of possessing and not possessing at the same time? The pain consumed him, but he rejoiced in his torment, knowing at least that his other self would always be faithful to him, no matter what (GRAVES, 2008, p. 341).

Between 1914 and 1923 Freud elaborated the so-called second topic of the psychic apparatus, and one of the central conceptual changes was the theory of narcissism. At the age of 58, he wrote and published the text "On Narcissism: An Introduction"/1914. In it, he developed his theory on this subject, emphasizing it in perversion and psychosis. It was even in psychosis that Freud began to question how the constitution of the self occurs.

Initially, Freud conceptualized narcissism as a possibility for understanding homosexual choices (text by Schreber/1911), later calling it an important developmental phase, where the self is constructed as a unit (HORNSTEIN, 1989). Freud (1916/1996, v. XIV, p. 81) states "... a localization of the libido that deserves to be described as narcissism would perhaps be present to a much greater extent, and might even claim a place in the regular course of human sexual development".

Narcissism corresponds to the child's libidinal investment in himself, and later in other objects. Freud (1916/1996, v.XIV, p.83) continues "...there is an original libidinal cathexis of the ego, part of which is later transmitted to objects, but which fundamentally persists and is related to the object cathexis...". Hornstein (1989, p.154) describes it thus: "Narcissism is defined, then, as a stage of libidinal development, of the development of the self and of object relations. In it, the self is invested as an object, and this investment is essential for its constitution."

Mucida (2006, p.98) points out that "Like Narcissus, that 'flame that feeds itself', narcissism imposes a protection or defense mechanism against the holes brought about by the encounter with reality".

Psychoanalytic theory argues that the subject is not born with a constituted self. Hornstein (2008, p.28) states that "the ego is a construction, a conquest. It doesn't exist at the beginning, but becomes so, with different structures, with different strengths". Garcia-Roza (2008, p.199) points out that "the ego is not an original reality and neither can narcissism be original", in other words, it is in the relationship with the other that narcissism occurs. Freud (1916/1996, v. XIV, p.84) states that:

> (...) we are destined to assume that a unit comparable to the ego cannot exist in the individual from the start; the ego has to be developed. The auto-erotic instincts, however, are there from the start, and it is therefore necessary for something to be added to auto-eroticism - a new psychic action - in order to bring about narcissism.

Still on the constitution of the self, Hornstein (1989, p.156) points out that:

> (...) the self must be adequately narcissized from the parents in order to be constituted. So the sexuality-self-conservation opposition is not simple, but there is also a second opposition, which is the libido of the self-libido of the object. And he says that narcissism is the libidinal complement of self-conservation, which, taken literally, means that in order for there to be self-conservation, the self must have been narcissized.

However, there is an earlier, preparatory stage of narcissism that needs to be pointed out - auto-eroticism. In the text "Three Essays on the Theory of Sexuality"/1905, that is, nine years before the publication of the text "Introduction to Narcissism", Freud addresses the subject of auto-eroticism, when he talks about the pleasure the child feels when suckling at the mother's breast. His satisfaction goes beyond the milk he receives, he stays much longer than necessary to feed himself, in a clear demonstration of delight, showing how much the baby's mouth is an erogenous zone that provides pleasure. "The most outstanding feature of this sexual practice is that the drive is not directed towards another person; it is satisfied in the body itself, it is auto-erotic" (FREUD, 1905/1996, v. VII, p. 171).

Garcia-Roza (2008, p.99) points out that "the term... (auto-eroticism)... is taken up by Freud... to characterize an original state of infantile sexuality prior to narcissism, in which the sexual drive, linked to an organ or to the excitement of an erogenous zone, finds satisfaction without resorting to an external object".

The constitution of the self is the passage from auto-eroticism to primary narcissism. Primary narcissism is formed in the symbiosis between mother and baby, in other words, here the self is idealized, it is the ideal-self, initially formed by the parents. When the parents "become pregnant" their narcissism resumes, Freud (1916/1996, v. XIV p.97) points out that "if we pay attention to the attitude of affectionate parents towards their children, we must recognize that it is a revival and reproduction of their own narcissism, which they have long since abandoned".

Starting from the symbiotic relationship between mother and baby, considering that the mother took care of him with pleasure, respecting him as a subject (and not as an extension of her own body) allowing the necessary oedipal cut (represented by intruders such as the father, work, mother's friends, etc.), the disturbance in the baby's primary narcissism arises. In other words, the "intruder" causes the necessary reorganization of the baby, who realizes that he isn't everything to his mother, giving rise to secondary narcissism, which now follows the path of identification, in other words, the ideal of the self will be formed from castration, the law and social values (HORNSTEIN, 1989).

According to Laplanche (2001, p.290) "primary narcissism designates an early state in which the child invests all its libido in itself. Secondary narcissism designates a return to the ego of the libido withdrawn from its object investments".

Parental love is the basis of the baby's narcissism, i.e. the formation of the self, which can develop self-esteem or self-preservation. In his translation of Freud's work, Hanns (2004, p.108) states that

> (...) we are affirming that the human being has two primordial sexual objects: himself and the woman who takes care of him, and with this we are presupposing that in every human being there is a primary narcissism, which can eventually manifest itself in a dominant way in his choice of object.

In the formation of the self, during primary narcissism, two possible object choices arise - anaclitic objects (transference from primary narcissism to object narcissism) and narcissistic objects (search for oneself in love objects).

Regarding objective choices, Garcia-Roza (2008, p. 201-202) points out that:

> The anaclitic type of choice (Anlehnungstypus) is characterized by the fact that the choice of love object falls on people who reproduce the model of the parental figures, insofar as they provide the child with nourishment and protection (...) The anaclitic type of choice results from the support of the sexual impulses over the impulses of self-preservation (...)....) therefore occurs in a double register: that of the impulses, in which the sexual impulses are supported by the impulses of self-preservation; and that of the objects, whose choice is made according to the model of the maternal breast, which is constituted as the first object of sexual satisfaction.
>
> The narcissistic type of choice is one that takes the person themselves as its model, that is, the object is chosen according to the image and likeness of the individual themselves and not taking the mother as its model.

Regarding the construction of the self, Goldfarb (1998, p.14) states that "the subject is the product of an encounter, of an articulation between interiority and exteriority, and this is not only the foundation of subjectivity, but also constitutes the field where the objects of its satisfaction are found".

2.2 Oedipus complex

Laius, king of Thebes, distressed at not being able to have children with his wife Jocasta, secretly consulted the oracle at Delphi. The oracle told him that a son would be the worst misfortune of his life; any child he had with Jocasta would become his murderer. From that moment on, he refuses Jocasta. Without understanding what was happening, Jocasta got him drunk and after nine months the boy was born. "Laius snatched him from his nurse's arms, pierced his feet with a nail and, tying them together, abandoned him on Mount Citeron" (GRAVES, 2008, p. 436).

A shepherd found him and took him to the kings of Corinth, King Polybus and Queen Peribea, who adopted him since they couldn't have children. One day a young Corinthian told Oedipus that he looked nothing like his parents. Oedipus went to consult the oracle at Delphi to find out what the future held for him: "Get away from the altar, you wretch! - he shouted in disgust - you will kill your father and marry your mother!" (GRAVES, 2008, p. 436).

Oedipus decides to leave Corinth. On the narrow road between Delphi and Dulis, Oedipus and Laius meet and argue. Oedipus kills Laius' charioteer with a spear and the latter is dragged to his death by his horses.

On arriving in Thebes, Oedipus deciphers the riddle of the Sphinx, ridding the city of the monster. In gratitude, the Thebans acclaimed Oedipus king, and he married Jocasta, unaware that she was his mother. He had children with Jocasta. On consulting the oracle again, Oedipus discovers that it was he who killed King Laius, his father, and that his wife was also his mother. Jocasta commits suicide by jumping from the top of the rock like the sphinx. Oedipus pierces his own eyes, goes blind and dies alone (GRAVES, 2008).

Freud theorized the Oedipus complex after several reports from his patients and his own self-analysis. There was no specific text that dealt clearly with this phase. His theory, in a nutshell, was that the son "falls in love" with the parent of the opposite sex and desires to kill the parent of the same sex, thus taking his place.

This event occurs between the ages of 3 and 5 and forms the self, being experienced differently by boys and girls. It is the basis of their sexuality and defines their psychic structure - neurotic, psychotic or paranoid. According to Násio (2007, p.67) "the problem of solving the Oedipus is the origin of our adult sexuality and, beyond that, the origin of our countless neurotic sufferings".

Hornstein (1989, p.185) points out that:

> The structuring of subjectivity is produced through the Oedipus, since the whole history of development is linked to the Oedipal scenario: the primary scene (as a question about origin), birth, the relationship with the breast, the constitution of the self (as an individualizing separate), the oedipal triangle, latency (as entry into the cultural world), puberty (as the re-emergence of the problem of sexual identity), adolescence (as the separating mourning of parents), the choice of object, the establishment of a couple relationship and the passage to motherhood and fatherhood.

Laplanche (2001, p.77) states that:

> (...) according to Freud, the apogee of the Oedipus complex is experienced between the ages of three and five... It is revived at puberty and is overcome with greater or lesser success in a special type of object choice... The Oedipus complex plays a fundamental role in the structuring of the personality and the orientation of human desire... Freud never presented a systematic exposition of the Oedipus complex.

2.3 The self and ageing

The question arises: and in old age, where is it possible to identify characteristics of the formation of the self, in other words, narcissism and the Oedipus complex? As we get older, certain resources are built up (individually) with the aim of avoiding and denying the human finitude that is so evident with ageing. Death is undoubtedly the greatest certainty that the ego wants to avoid. Bianchi (1993, p.77) points out that "(...) we find at this point (old age) the attempt made by the I to survive itself by identifying with an entity more durable than itself: progeny, work, institution, soul, etc".

Increasing bodily, psychological and social changes are taking place, and they can represent a blow to self-esteem, a castration of the self, causing decline and a feeling of inferiority. The body weakens rapidly, requiring ever greater care, medication and diets. Mourning is present on a daily basis (loss of beauty, health, retirement, marriage of children, birth of grandchildren, financial independence of children, deaths of people close to them, etc.), the mind betrays you, and death is the only certainty and it's fast approaching. "The traces of loss, of the dulling of curiosity and desire, attest to ageing" (BIANCHI, 1993, p. 89).

The exaltation of beauty, youth and production capacity leads to the devaluation of growing old, nullifying its condition as a desiring being. There is a lack of a valued symbolic place for the old, where pleasure can take place, otherwise there will be a denarcation of the subject. In other words, a lack of investment from the environment in the subject and vice versa, "which prevents the elaboration of the loss and causes a growing impoverishment of the affective life. Often, the response to this process is depression or dementia as a defense of the last narcissistic bastion" (GOLDFARB, 1998, p.14).

There is also the possibility of the subject directing his libido, all his energy, towards himself, turning his attention to his needs, thus explaining the increase in his narcissism (COSTA, 1998).

Mucida (2006, p.99) points out that:

> In old age, the encounter with the reality of a body that is changing, marked by an anticipated image announcing the irreparable nature of some changes - an image that is not always easy to bear - as well as other losses concerning the possibilities of social ties - which the ideal of the self could sustain - all this can promote a return to the ideal self represented by the identification with objects. Thus, the lack of symbolic traits introjected by the ideal of the self, through which the subject could be loved, in the absence of an ideal that can mediate between the self and narcissism and in the lack of sublimatory lakes, can lead to both attachment to objects and the predominance of hatred, as well as temporary or non-transient depressive states. What common sense often caricatures as 'old man's mania' - excessive attachment to objects ... seems to us to be an attempt to maintain a certain consistency of self.

The Argentinian psychogeriatrician and psychoanalyst Salvarezza (*apud* COSTA, 1998, p.140), who studies the relationship between narcissism and ageing, states that "the subject's valuation of himself is placed within a scale of values at the highest end of which is the ideal and at the lowest the negative of said ideal. The position on this scale gives the measure of self-esteem".

Costa (1998) demonstrates Salvarezza's theory with a figure, which she considers relevant to reproduce:

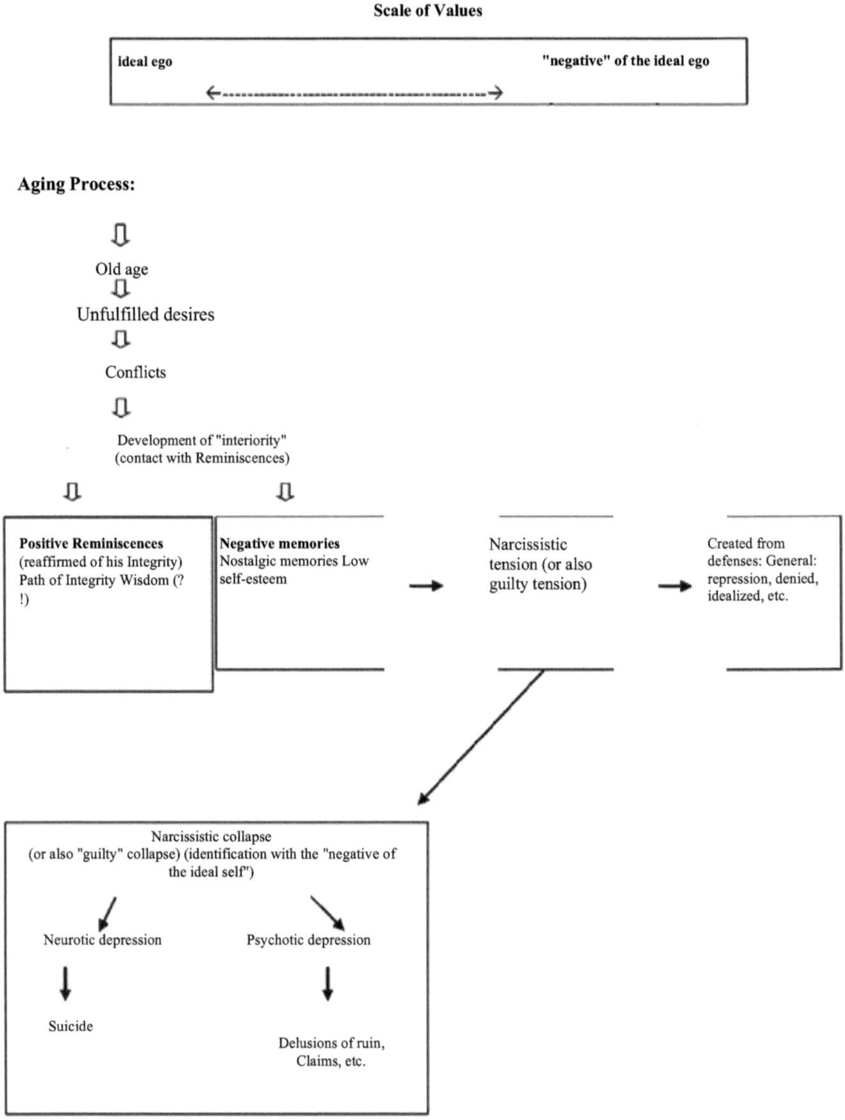

Figure 1 - Ego and aging.
Source: Salvarezza (*apud* COSTA, 1998, p.149).

Salvarezza (*apud* COSTA, 1998) considers that the majority of elderly people suffer from some form of depression, which led him to investigate this issue. His studies on narcissism in the elderly are based on the aspect of self-esteem and the structural relationship with the concept of the ideal. When the elderly realize that they can no longer satisfy their desires, they enter into conflict and withdraw from the external world, increasing their internal reflections and returning to memories of the past (interiority).

Salvarezza (*apud* COSTA, 1998) argues that when older people make more use of reminiscences, they have less risk of becoming mentally ill. Reminiscences are the bridges that link the past and the present. When they are positive, there is a reaffirmation of self-esteem, the individual feels at peace and accompanies their finitude with wisdom and integrity. However, when reminiscences are negative, and the past is brought up through painful - nostalgic - memories, and the elderly person believes that they have lost everything to the young, they feel that they no longer have time to remake their lives and death is approaching "the ideal self is represented as unattainable, and their sense of self-worth is severely damaged" (SALVAREZZA, *apud* COSTA, 1998, p.145).

Everyone has an ideal ego that guides their attitudes throughout life. Those who grow old based on positive reminiscences try to be close to this ideal ego on the scale of values. Those who move towards nostalgia are closer to the "negative" of the ideal ego, which can cause a narcissistic collapse with a fate linked to depression, according to the scheme mentioned above (COSTA, 1998).

Costa (1998) also mentions Erik Erikson's Epigenetic Theory of the Life

Cycle. In this theory, the life cycle is divided into eight stages: the first six relate to the personality from childhood to adulthood and the last two deal with ageing.

Stage 7 covers the 40 to 65 age group. These are people who are moving towards "productivity" or "stagnation". When they turn to productivity, they show themselves to be fertile and have the need to make themselves useful to others, in a movement of giving themselves to their offspring in a direct or indirect way. They want to teach, care for, guide and support the younger ones, playing a role in promoting the "maintenance of the world". The other possibility - stagnation - is accompanied by isolation, self-centered, impoverished and selfish individuals (COSTA, 1998).

Costa (1998) explains that stage 8 refers to subjects over 65 - ego integrity vs. despair. Here the result of the previous cycles is evident. Integrity is the fruit of personal maturation, built on triumphs and disappointments. It is the ability to accept oneself, overcoming inevitable physical changes, with the feeling of having succeeded prevailing. This attitude leads to wisdom, which is the ability to assimilate life's experiences well. Still on stage 8, Brink (1983, p.63) points out that "integrity is the acceptance of life in its entirety, in the face of the physical, social and perhaps even mental decline of old age, and in the face of the prospect of death itself".

The other possibility, despair, would be the experience of failure at this moment, coupled with the impossibility of change, since death is near. The feeling that life is now too short to achieve the desired wholeness prevails. The solutions commonly found by the ego range from phobias, unhappiness, hopelessness, depression (neurotic or psychotic) and suicide (COSTA, 1998).

On despair Brink (1983, p.63) states that:

> (...) individuals who have failed to do such a thing (live meaningfully the first years of life) find themselves enveloped in despair. This despair can be hidden behind loathing and contempt for others, or for the future generation, or blaming others for their failures in life. The deepest and final part of despair is that it would now be too late to start again and correct the past.

The authors cited in this section generally affirm the two possibilities of the self for aging, which were presented in Chapter 1 - wise or a hindrance. However, not from society's point of view, but from the individual's own, who can experience their old age in a productive/wise way, or dulled in themselves, devaluing themselves, finding a possible end in depression. "(...) the shadow of the object has fallen on the ego, and it can henceforth be judged by a special agent as if it were an object, the abandoned object" (FREUD, 1917/1996 v. XIV, p.254).

Chapter 3

3 DEPRESSION IN AGEING

In this monographic study, mourning and depression have been discussed on several occasions. Here, mourning corresponds to the loss of youth, health, employment, friends and family who pass away. And depression would be a possibility for the self in the face of human finitude, i.e. there is no more time to start again and now what is left does not satisfy.

Freud wrote "Mourning and Melancholia"/1917, a year after writing "Introduction to Narcissism"71916, which laid the foundations for his theory. In this text, Freud differentiates between mourning and melancholia (which would be depression). In mourning there is a chosen object that has been lost, and in melancholy the lost object is the self. "Mourning, in general, is the reaction to the loss of a loved one, the loss of some abstraction that has taken the place of a loved one, such as one's country, one's freedom or one's ideal... (FREUD, 1917/1996, v. XIV, p.249). In melancholia "one can recognize that there is a loss of a more ideal nature. The object may not really have died, but it has been lost as an object of love.

lost' (FREUD, 1917/1996, v. XIV, p.251).

In the text "Mourning and melancholy" Freud (1917/1996, v. XIV, p.250) defines melancholy as:

> The distinctive mental traits of melancholia are a profoundly painful despondency, a cessation of interest in the external world, a loss of the capacity to love, inhibition of any and all activity, and a diminishing of feelings of self-worth to the point where they find expression in self-recrimination and self-blame, culminating in a delusional expectation of punishment.

And he adds "the disturbance of self-esteem is absent in mourning; apart from that, however, the characteristics are the same" (FREUD, 1917/1996, v. XIV, p.250). In mourning, reality shows that the chosen object no longer exists, forcing the self to divest its libido of this object. "This demand provokes an understandable opposition - it is a well-known fact that people never willingly abandon a libidinal position, not even, in reality, when a substitute already beckons" (FREUD, 1917/1996, v. XIV, p.250). Therefore, mourning is temporary and untreatable, unlike depression.

Bion (*apud* Hornstein, 2008, p.49) points out that:

> Mourning is a polysemic term. It designates the psychic state in the face of a loss (it involves considering the nature of the person lost, the pre-existing relationship and the type of loss). It also designates a set of social behaviors, both individual and collective, following the death of a person. Finally, it designates a type of psychic work and its subjective changes.

The World Health Organization (WHO) states that 121 million people suffer from depression. Could depression be a modern-day plague[I] ?

People in a depressed mood have a loss of energy and interest, feelings of guilt, difficulty concentrating, loss of appetite and thoughts of death or suicide. They have a pessimistic view of themselves ("I'm worthless, I have no strength") and the world ("there is no future"), as well as a feeling of failure and impotence. There is a loss of the ability to experience pleasure, whatever that may be (HORNTEIN, 2008).

Bowlby (2004) highlights the possible relationship between childhood experiences and depressive disorders. He highlights three situations: the bitter experience of never having established a stable and secure relationship with one's parents (despite having made efforts to do so), the experience of repeatedly hearing how unworthy one was of being loved, or inconvenient, or incompetent and/or the person having suffered the actual loss of a parent (realization of the Oedipus), feeling

[I] Any epidemic with a large death toll. Mini Aurelio.

guilty for not having prevented it and, unconsciously, having wished for it. The three points made by the author bring up the concepts discussed in chapter 2 of this study - narcissism and the Oedipus complex.

Hornstein (2008, p.23) highlights the relationship between narcissism and depression: "Self-esteem comes from infantile narcissism and ideal achievements; it is a residue, but not a disposable one. Like rivers, self-esteem converges: a history, successes, the configuration of bonds, as well as projects (individual and collective) that feed the present from the future."

Kohut (*apud* COSTA, 1998) deals with the subject of depression in the context of narcissism, talking about ambition and the ideal. He explains: for this author, man should not deny his ambitions, his desire for power, his desire to shine, to join the ranks of the omnipotent. Instead of denying them, he should recognize and value these "narcissistic forces", as well as transforming the exhibitionist side into real feelings of self-esteem and pleasure in himself. The subject should also be able to allow themselves to admire great personalities, using them as models. He advocates conquering ideals in order to reduce the subject's vulnerability and narcissistic tensions.

> If the ideal is not achieved, the general tendency is for the ego to experience a feeling similar to nostalgia, rather than a narcissistic wound. On the other hand, when ambitions are not realized, narcissistic tensions occur and the ego can experience a sense of disappointment interspersed with shame, feelings of inferiority and frustration that can lead to what is known as "narcissistic mortification". (KOHUT, *apud* COSTA, 1998, p.148).

Kohut (*apud* COSTA, 1998) calls "narcissistic wound" the representation of disturbances in narcissistic balance, which are easy to recognize due to the painful embarrassment or shame that accompanies them and their ideational elaboration, known as feelings of inferiority or wounded self-love.

Hornstein (2008, p.48) points out that "depressives defend themselves at the sign of a frustrating response that could generate a narcissistic wound. For depressives, losses are a narcissistic wound. They illustrate how the ego is fed by others. The object configuration is usually variable".

Goldfarb (1998) talks about the importance of listening to reminiscences in the fight against depression in the elderly. The elderly use their reminiscences (fanciful or not) as a way of linking the present to the past, thereby accepting reality and outlining their own future. The amount of free libido that can't find objects to (re)invest will look for the image of its own self in the past. A self that serves as an anchor for this unknown moment close to death. Reminiscence has the constructive function of repetition as a sustainer of identity. It is the insistence of the subject's history. Otherwise, memories will be accompanied by sadness, about a lost object or the power of others (for example: youth), in other words, old age as a painful experience, incapable of choosing new objects.

Hornstein (2008) groups depressions into categories:

a. Mood and affective states: sadness, low self-esteem, self-reproach, loss of pleasure and interest, feeling of emptiness, apathy, anxiety, tension, irritability, various inhibitions;
b. Thinking: poor concentration, indecisiveness, guilt, pessimism, crises of ideals and values, suicidal thoughts;
c. Somatic manifestations: alteration of some function (insomnia, hypersomnia, increased or decreased appetite, decreased sex drive), body pain (headaches, back pain, joint pain) and visceral symptoms.

   (mainly gastrointestinal and cardiovascular).

All the categories mentioned illustrate how in depression the ego becomes poor and empty. Narcissistic investments and self-esteem disappear. The subject loses their value and importance.

Using the definitions of narcissism contained in Chapter 2 of this study, the aging self has the possibility of going down the path of depression. It is a way out of the inability to "live again", as well as the constant presence of death, evidenced by the body, by the reality that is imposed at this stage.

CONCLUSION

Throughout the research carried out for this monographic study, the relevance of the analytical process for the elderly became clear to this author. Not just in the sense of favoring the necessary adaptation to this vital phase, but, above all, to (re)signify the history of life, in the search for a more harmonious coexistence with the body, subjectivity and the social.

The possibility of (re)meaning one's own history favors the process of self-knowledge that humans are immersed in from birth. According to

Fonseca Filho (*apud*, Costa, 1998, p.151):

> The recognition of the self ... strictly speaking, is always present in the history of a human being. There are peaks, the most important of which, because it is basic, is the first, i.e. early childhood. The second peak is adolescence, and the third is the transition to senility. Man is constantly in this process of self-knowledge, which never comes to an end, because it is inexhaustible.

All the elaboration carried out in this study did not take into account the condition

the elderly. However, any kind of analytical treatment needs to include the subject's minimal lucidity. Costa (1998, p.155) points out that "ageing is the natural evolutionary process of life and old age is the condition of being old, which should not be seen as synonymous with old age or incapacity... most elderly people are in good health". Physical and mental.

As for psychoanalytic concepts, Freud, in 1898, (*apud* Mucida, 2006, p.186) stated that:

> Psychoanalytic therapy is not currently applicable to all cases. In my opinion, it has the following limitations: it requires a certain degree of maturity and understanding in patients and is therefore not suitable for young people or mentally weak or uneducated adults. It fails with elderly people, because the treatment would take up so much time, due to the accumulation of material, that in the end they would have reached a period of life in which they attached no value to nervous health..."

However, throughout his work, Freud always stressed the need for psychoanalytic research to continue. The post-Freudians demonstrated the importance of the analytical clinic for children and psychotics. Why not with the old? Brink (1983, p.61) points out that:

> Although several psychoanalytically oriented therapists have succeeded in working with the elderly, the vast majority of psychoanalysts have not been inspired by these attempts to the point of applying Freudian insights to geriatrics. As a result, most psychoanalysts have never treated a patient in their last years of life.

In his text "The unconscious"/1915, Freud highlighted the timeless nature of the unconscious, i.e. there is no chronological age for the unconscious, a thesis also defended by Mucida in his book: The subject does not age. Freud (1915/1996, v.XIV, p.192) stated that "The processes of the Ics. system are timeless. They are timeless; that is, they are not temporally ordered, they do not change with the passage of time; they have absolutely no reference to time".

In defense of an analysis of the elderly, Abraham (*apud,* Mucida, 2006, p.187 and Brink, 1983) points out that the most important thing is not chronological age: "it can equally be said that the age of the neurosis is more important than the life of the neurotic".

The only rule Freud stipulated for analysis was free association. This is entirely possible for lucid elderly people. This author disagrees with the recurrent assertion that the analysis of the elderly is the same as that of other adults. Human finitude becomes very apparent after the age of 60 and I believe that this fact alters the entire dynamics of the functioning of the ego, as was demonstrated in chapter 2.

This author goes so far as to say that, as old age is something of the order of reality, it can mobilize in the analyst their ghosts of finitude, their mourning and their human incapacity to regain "lost time". "The real of old age lurks around us in different ways" (MUCIDA, 2006, p.186). Freud, in my opinion, is an example of this: he denied the possibility of analysis in the elderly and produced until his death in a tireless quest to deny his illness and his finitude.

The general aim of this study was to investigate the possible relationship between narcissism and ageing. Throughout chapter 2, the constitution of the self was demonstrated, from auto-eroticism, narcissism and the Oedipus complex. The importance of maternal love in the initial constitution, object choice and the necessary castration for entry into the real world was highlighted.

Brink (1983) highlights the existence of an inverted Oedipus complex in old age, where the elderly become dependent on their adult children and transfer to them part of the libido originally invested in the old person's biological parents, functioning as a regression. This author interpreted the crises of the last years of life as a narcissistic trauma, due to castration anxiety - of beauty, health, social life, independence, etc.

Prior to chapter 2, the author considered it relevant to give a brief social history of the roles occupied by the old man - wise or a nuisance. Sigmund Freud's life story was used to illustrate the construction of the wise old man. According to Salvarreza and Erik Erikson (chapter 2), Freud was always in search of the ideal ego and ego integrity. Through his theoretical production, he preserved his ego, became immortal, and theorized very important works for psychoanalysis after his 60th birthday, as has already been shown. In a clear movement of "usefulness" and transmission of knowledge. Not even cancer could stop Freud.

If on the one hand the old sage was exemplified by Sigmund Freud, on the other hand the old hindrance was exemplified by depression, a pathology that is very present today. However, it should *be* pointed out that in some cases, depression can be "disguised". It's very common to hear (from common sense) that men are less depressed. That's a mistake. Common examples of male depression include forgetting to take medication, not going to appointments and not following medical advice, not respecting diets, as well as alcoholism and drug use. These cases are not initially diagnosed as depression because their attitude is not reflected in dullness and silence, but in a violent attitude towards others and themselves, in this daily and "homeopathic" suicide (HORNTEIN, 2008).

I emphasize the importance of listening to this subject who is often frightened by his own aging, as if it were something that happened "outside" him. Analysis can be an important tool in understanding this process that we are immersed in from birth. It is up to the analyst to listen to these losses, pains and bereavements faced by the over-60s, not with the aim of transcending death and inexorable time, but by understanding and giving voice to this complex and sometimes frightening other.

This study is just the beginning of an investigation into possible psychoanalytic work with the elderly. Further complementary studies are needed to build knowledge about ageing from a psychoanalytic perspective.

REFERENCES

BIANCHI, Henri. **The self and time: psychoanalysis of time and ageing**. Sao Paulo: Casa do Psicólogo, 1993.

BREGER, Louis. **Freud, the hidden side of the visionary**. Sao Paulo: Editora Manole, 2002.

BRINK, L.T. **Psicoterapia geriátrica**. Rio de Janeiro: Imago, 1983.

BOWBY, John. **Loss: grief and depression.** Volume 3 of the "attachment and loss" trilogy. Sao Paulo: Martins, 2004.

COSTA, Elisabeth Maria Sene. **Gerontodrama - Old age on stage: clinical and psychodramatic studies on ageing and old age**. Sao Paulo: Ágora, 1998.

EDMUNDSON, Mark. **Freud's death: the legacy of his last days**.
Translation: Luciano Tiago. Rio de Janeiro: Odisséia Editorial, 2009.

FREUD, Sigmund. In Brazilian standard edition of the complete psychological works of Sigmund Freud. **Three Essays on Sexuality - autoeroticism**. Rio de Janeiro: Imago. v. VII. 1905/1996.

FREUD, Sigmund. In Brazilian standard edition of the complete psychological works of Sigmund Freud. **Totem and Taboo**. Rio de Janeiro: Imago. v. XIII. 1914/1996.

FREUD, Sigmund. In Brazilian standard edition of the complete psychological works of Sigmund Freud. **The unconscious**. Rio de Janeiro: Imago. v. XIV. 1915/1996.

FREUD, Sigmund. In Brazilian Standard Edition of the Complete Psychological Works of Sigmund Freud. **On Narcissism: an introduction**. Rio de Janeiro: Imago. v. XIV. 1916/1996.

FREUD, Sigmund. In Brazilian Standard Edition of the Complete Psychological Works of Sigmund Freud. **Mourning and melancholy**. Rio de Janeiro: Imago. v. XIV. 1917/1996.

GARCIA-ROZA, Luiz Alfredo. **Freud and the unconscious**. 23ª edition. Rio de Janeiro: Jorge Zahar, 2008.

GOLDFARB, Delia Catullo. **Body, time and ageing**. Sao Paulo: Casa do psicólogo, 1998.

GRAVES, Robert. **The great book of Greek myths**. Sao Paulo: Ediouro, 2008.

HANNS, Luiz Alberto. Psychological works of Sigmund Freud. **Writings on the psychology of the unconscious (1915-1920).** Vol. 2. Rio de Janeiro: Imago, 2006.

HORNSTEIN, Luis. **Introduction to Psychoanalysis**. Sao Paulo: Editora Escuta, 1989.

HORNSTEIN, Luis. **Depression. Affections and moods of living**. Sao Paulo: Via Lettera: Center for Psychoanalytic Studies, 2008.

KAMKHAGI, Dorli. **Psychoanalysis and old age: on the clinic of growing old**. Sao Paulo: Via Lettera, 2008.

LAPLANCHE, Jean; PONTALIS. **Vocabulary of psychoanalysis**. 4ª edition. Sao Paulo: Martins Fontes, 2001.

MUCIDA, Ángela. **The subject doesn't age - psychoanalysis and old age.** Auténtica: Belo Horizonte, 2006.

NASIO. J.-D. **The pleasure of reading Freud**. Rio de Janeiro: Jorge Zahar, 1999.

NASIO. J.-D. Oedipus. **The complex from which no child escapes.** Rio de Janeiro: Jorge Zahar, 2007.

MIX
Papier aus verantwortungsvollen Quellen
Paper from responsible sources
FSC® C105338

Printed by Books on Demand GmbH, Norderstedt / Germany